100% UNOFFICIAL
APEX
LEGENDS

ESSENTIAL GUIDE

DEAN

First published in Great Britain in 2019 by Dean,
an imprint of Egmont UK Limited
The Yellow Building, 1 Nicholas Road, London, W11 4AN
www.egmont.co.uk

Written by Daniel Lipscombe
Designed by Design Button Ltd.

Copyright © Egmont UK Limited 2019

ISBN 978 1 4052 9597 0
70770/001
Printed in Italy

ONLINE SAFETY FOR YOUNGER FANS

Spending time online is great fun! Here are a few simple rules to help younger
fans stay safe and keep the internet a great place to spend time.
For more advice and guidance, please see pages 62-63 of this book.

- Never give out your real name – don't use it as your username.
- Never give out any of your personal details.
- Never tell anybody which school you go to or how old you are.
- Never tell anybody your password, except a parent or guardian.
- Be aware that you must be 13 or over to create an account on many sites. Always check
the site policy and ask a parent or guardian for permission before registering.
- Always tell a parent or guardian if something is worrying you.

Stay safe online. Any website addresses listed in this book are correct at the
time of going to print. However, Egmont is not responsible for content hosted by
third parties. Please be aware that online content can be subject to change and
websites can contain content that is unsuitable for children. We advise that
all children are supervised when using the internet.

Egmont takes its responsibility to the planet and its inhabitants very seriously.
We aim to use papers from well-managed forests run by responsible suppliers.

100% UNOFFICIAL

APEX
LEGENDS

ESSENTIAL GUIDE

CONTENTS

WHAT IS APEX LEGENDS?

Apex Legends is a fast-paced Battle Royale game developed by Respawn Entertainment that is taking the world by storm and knocking others in the genre from the top spot. Apex Legends dropped from nowhere to the surprise of gamers across the world and quickly began breaking records and setting new standards.

Within 30 days of release, the game surpassed 50 million players and shows no sign of slowing down. In that time, players placed over 31 billion pings, used 1.23 billion ultimate abilities and respawned teammates over 170 million times. It's quite likely that if you're reading this book you will have dabbled with Apex Legends, but if you haven't or are still finding your feet, we've put together a brief overview of how to play this new blockbuster game.

Apex Legends differs from other Battle Royale titles in that players choose from specific characters who each have unique abilities and form a team of three, but otherwise plays like others in the genre – there's one map, you drop from the sky to land where you choose, loot buildings and chests for gear and aim to finish in the top spot.

The game is built with teams in mind as you join up with two other players to form a squad – and whether you're playing with friends or randoms, this means teamwork and communication are key.

Let's drop in, load-up and learn everything about King's Canyon.

HOW TO PLAY

A match of Apex Legends takes place in King's Canyon and lasts for up to 30 minutes. Once you and your squad drop into the map, players must search for the best weapons and items in order to eliminate the opposition and become the last team standing.

Each Apex Legends match is played in rounds, and a game can last a maximum of eight rounds, though that's very rare. Each round is broken down into two sections: waiting and closing. In the waiting time, you can see where The Ring will move to next and during the closing time, The Ring shrinks and makes the playing area smaller

In order to ensure players battle each other rather than stay in one place, The Ring closes and moves around the map. Being caught outside this ring means only one thing – damage. The Ring causes damage every 1.5 seconds, so move fast otherwise you'll be eliminated.

Apex Legends is currently available for PlayStation 4, XBOX One and PC. Here are the control schemes for each platform.

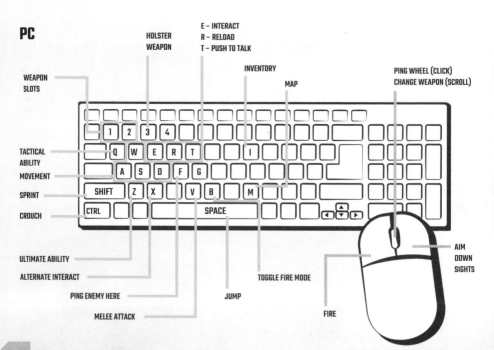

PC

HOLSTER WEAPON

E – INTERACT
R – RELOAD
T – PUSH TO TALK

INVENTORY

MAP

PING WHEEL (CLICK)
CHANGE WEAPON (SCROLL)

WEAPON SLOTS

TACTICAL ABILITY

MOVEMENT

SPRINT

CROUCH

ULTIMATE ABILITY

ALTERNATE INTERACT

PING ENEMY HERE

MELEE ATTACK

JUMP

TOGGLE FIRE MODE

FIRE

AIM DOWN SIGHTS

XBOX ONE

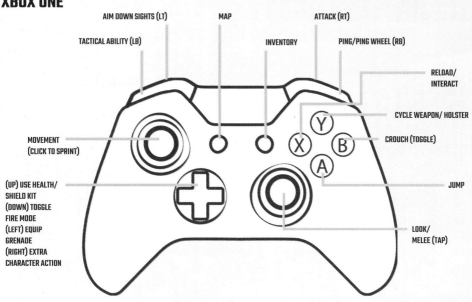

AIM DOWN SIGHTS (LT)
MAP
ATTACK (RT)

TACTICAL ABILITY (LB)
INVENTORY
PING/PING WHEEL (RB)

RELOAD/
INTERACT

CYCLE WEAPON/ HOLSTER

MOVEMENT
(CLICK TO SPRINT)
CROUCH (TOGGLE)

(UP) USE HEALTH/
SHIELD KIT
(DOWN) TOGGLE
FIRE MODE
(LEFT) EQUIP
GRENADE
(RIGHT) EXTRA
CHARACTER ACTION
JUMP

LOOK/
MELEE (TAP)

PLAYSTATION 4

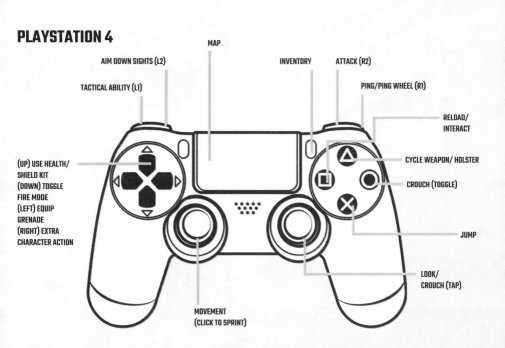

MAP

AIM DOWN SIGHTS (L2)
INVENTORY
ATTACK (R2)

TACTICAL ABILITY (L1)
PING/PING WHEEL (R1)

RELOAD/
INTERACT

(UP) USE HEALTH/
SHIELD KIT
(DOWN) TOGGLE
FIRE MODE
(LEFT) EQUIP
GRENADE
(RIGHT) EXTRA
CHARACTER ACTION
CYCLE WEAPON/ HOLSTER

CROUCH (TOGGLE)

JUMP

LOOK/
CROUCH (TAP)

MOVEMENT
(CLICK TO SPRINT)

KING'S CANYON

There's just one gigantic map available in Apex Legends – King's Canyon. This open and varied arena has plenty of areas to explore and vantage points that can turn the tide of battle. No matter where you land, the rarity of awesome loot you find will be random. The map can give you an idea of what you'll find at each location by highlighting the tier next to the mini-map.

1 Landing between Artillery and Cascades will give you a shot at lots of loot crates, and also provides the option of reaching taller buildings for a good vantage point, or the wide open area down below.

2 Skull Town regularly offers mid- or high-tier loot and features a great circular defence to keep your team safe as you tool up.

3 If you want the high ground and the ability to scope out what others are doing, then drop towards The Pit and stick the landing on top of the peaks.

4 Airbase is a tempting balance of risk and reward. While the loot is often excellent, it's perched on the edge of the map, which limits movement options and often puts you in danger of being caught outside The Ring.

5 Repulsor is a bit of a rat's maze, offering both loot and plenty of hidey-holes, including underground tunnels. A great place for traps and ambushes.

6 Swamps is as chaotic as it looks from the sky, with lots of little pocket areas to set up flanking movements ... or be ambushed. Lots of communication is needed in this area.

7 If you don't mind landing on the outskirts, away from the action, then Relay often pays out with decent guns and items. You might be on danger of being caught by The Ring here though (see pages 10-11 for more information on The Ring).

8 Shotgun specialists will love Slum Lakes for its tightly-packed corridors and little houses. No need for long-range weapons here, but keep your eye out for supply crates.

THE RING

The Ring is a harmful barrier that closes slowly over time to push players towards each other and force squads into battle. Not only does this keep the mayhem flowing, but it encourages you to make a trip to different areas of the map. The starting position of The Ring is random, but after a few games you'll be better able to read how The Ring will move across King's Canyon.

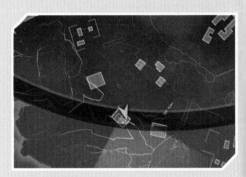

A match of Apex Legends can be easily broken down into eight rounds, meaning The Ring will move eight times during a match, getting smaller each time, unless the required number of players are eliminated first. It's very unlikely you will see a match reach round eight as most halt about halfway through.

TIP

Some characters can use their abilities to reach The Ring faster than others. Bloodhound's ultimate will increase speed, as will Wraith's 'Into the Void' ability. If you have Pathfinder on your team, you'll know where The Ring will move anyway.

You'll have around a minute and a half from boarding the transport ship to land and loot before The Ring appears. If you're caught beyond The Ring, you will start to take damage every second and a half. Both the waiting and closing periods will decrease with each subsequent round, whereas the damage caused will increase. Consult the chart below to see how long each round lasts.

ROUND	WAITING	CLOSING	DAMAGE PER 1.5 SECONDS
1	4 minutes	2 minutes 30 seconds	1
2	3 minutes 30 seconds	1 minute 3 seconds	2
3	3 minutes	35 seconds	5
4	2 minutes 15 seconds	28 seconds	5
5	2 minutes	18 seconds	10
6	1 minute 30 seconds	5 seconds	10
7	2 minutes	6.5 seconds	10
8	20 seconds	1 second	10

WHERE AND HOW TO DROP

You've scanned King's Canyon, have an idea of where you want to drop and, of course, you want to be the first to get your boots on the ground. Apex Legends handles dropping into the battlefield differently from other Battle Royales. You can simply hold a direction and point your nose towards your destination, however, with some easy to learn techniques, you can reach the ground even faster. Make sure your team can keep up!

JUMPMASTER

Once you've selected your character, one of your team will be selected as the Jumpmaster. This is the person who will control when you leave the ship and the descent to the ground. If you're selected as Jumpmaster, it's worth waiting for your team to confirm where they'd like to land, as some players will have preferences for certain areas. You won't have long to do this, so offer a few options and ask them to ping their chosen zone.

> ### TIP
> Use the ping system if you can't voice-chat with your team. You can easily add a ping to a teammate's marker to confirm a landing spot (see page 54 for ping info).

WAVE-DROP

It's tempting to just dive straight for the ground, which is fine if you're directly over your desired dropzone. To reach further away, try these steps to do a wave-drop:

- Drop straight downwards vertically until you reach around 145 – 150 on your speed gauge.

- Once you hit 145, level yourself out and glide towards where you want to land until you slow down to 130.

- Repeat to get back to a speed of 145-150, then drop directly downwards when you're above your target.

This method allows you to travel horizontal distances much faster than if you were to just point yourself where you want to go and glide all the way.

PREPARE FOR LANDING

You may want to land close together, but those opening minutes are about finding the best gear. If you land too close to your teammates, you'll end up squabbling over weapons. Try to land a short distance away from one another to maximise your loot gains.

TEAM PLAYER

As Jumpmaster, you'll want to focus on reaching the ideal landing area. If you weren't selected, then you can still help out. Keep your eyes peeled for other teams – each one leaves a coloured trail behind them as they fall, so monitor the surrounding areas and ping the points where they're about to land. The Jumpmaster may alter the course to avoid an early battle with an enemy team.

MEET THE LEGENDS

Apex comes with a cast of colourful heroes, otherwise known as Legends. Each character has their own set of quirks, attitudes and abilities that affect the way you play with them. We're here to guide you through the many options available, so that you can pick the character that matches your play-style. Whether you're an all-action frontline-fighter or prefer to sit back and help your team from a distance, there's a Legend for you.

We encourage you to try out each member of the roster, because, while they each have strengths, they also have weaknesses. It's worth keeping in mind that each Legend available has the same health, movement speed and attack power. The element that sets them apart from each other is their set of skills.

Over the next few pages, we'll show you each Legend and break down their skills while looking at how each member can fit into a squad that must work as a team. We've included a Class Title to each character so that you can see at a glance if they're the one for you and we've included a few tips as to which weapons suit each member.

BANGALORE

BLOODHOUND

CAUSTIC

GIBRALTAR

LIFELINE

MIRAGE

OCTANE

PATHFINDER

WRAITH

BANGALORE

SUPPORT

PROFILE

Real Name: Anita Williams
Age: 35

Bangalore is a professional soldier, born and bred. Her family were soldiers, so she followed in their footsteps. Anita's mission is to find her family on the way back from the battlefront, using all the skills at her disposal.

STRENGTHS

Bangalore's speed boost is a great passive ability for escaping battle or moving behind an enemy position.

WEAKNESSES

Don't rely on her ultimate ability for taking out enemies, it's best used to suppress their movement.

SKILLS

Double Time (Passive)
When taking fire from the enemy, sprinting allows Bangalore to move faster for a brief period of time.

Smoke Launcher (Active)
Bangalore fires a grenade that explodes into a wall of smoke on impact, reducing the field of vision of your enemies.

Rolling Thunder (Ultimate)
Bangalore's ultimate ability allows you to call in an artillery strike by throwing down a signal beacon. The airstrike slowly and destructively sweeps across the map, totally decimating everything in its path.

HOW TO USE

While Bangalore may look like she can deal lots of damage, she's best when providing backup to more aggressive Legends. Her ability to move faster is ideal for reaching a downed teammate and her smoke launcher provides great cover. These abilities combine to make Bangalore an effective helper in sticky situations.

Her ultimate, while destructive, does require precision. In order to drop the beacon to damage an enemy, you'll need to get close, so communication is key. Your squad will need to pin down the enemy once the beacon is deployed to stop your target from running away. It can also be used to flush an enemy from cover and towards your team for quick elimination.

BLOODHOUND

HUNTER

PROFILE

Real Name: Unknown
Age: Unknown

Little is known about Bloodhound other than his almost supernatural ability to track opponents to the ends of the Earth. With a connection to the Norse Gods, nobody knows if Bloodhound is part God or just in league with them.

STRENGTHS

Being able to see and ping opponents through walls is a valuable ability for the whole squad.

WEAKNESSES

Eye of the AllFather is a double-edged sword as it also allows enemies to see your location.

SKILLS

Tracker (Passive)
Bloodhound's passive is great for leading you to an enemy location, as you will see clues left behind by your foes.

Eye of the AllFather (Active)
Use this to briefly reveal traps, clues and enemies in the surrounding area. This means you can let your team know what's about.

Beast of the Hunt (Ultimate)
Utilising Bloodhounds ultimate ability greatly enhances your senses so you can spot enemies more easily. You also move faster, so you can use your advanced senses to plan and execute a deadly sneak attack.

HOW TO USE

Bloodhound is a hunter and excels in tracking down and eliminating enemies. There's no point in having all those tracking skills so you can sit back and watch your teammates rack up the kills. His abilities allow him to actively pursue others, scout areas and place pings on enemies, alerting everyone to possible threats and targets.

He's a great starting character to use as he encourages players to read the map in more detail as well as practise comms through voice chat or the ping system. Bloodhound's 35-second ultimate ability lends itself to either offence or defence, allowing for speedy flanking movement or a fast fallback if things get too dangerous.

CAUSTIC

TOXIC TRAPPER

PROFILE

Real Name: Alexander Nox
Age: 48

Alexander was once a successful scientist tasked with protecting crops using a form of pesticide. In order to improve the formula, he experimented on living creatures, warping his morality. Nox is presumed dead, but Caustic is alive and well.

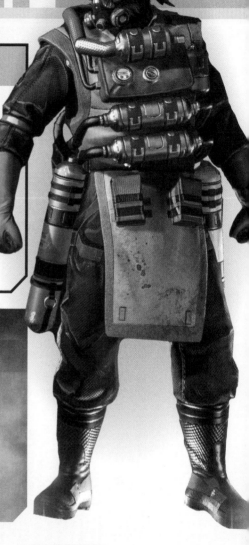

STRENGTHS

Caustic's ultimate has two benefits: it damages enemies slowly and reveals their positions on the map.

WEAKNESSES

Traps are situational, meaning that they can be avoided and won't necessarily result in damage.

SKILLS

Nox Vision (Passive)
When enemies move through any of Caustic's gas traps, they're highlighted on the map so you can see their position.

Nox Gas Trap (Active)
Caustic places up to six lethal canisters, which release a deadly gas when shot at or triggered by enemy movement.

Nox Gas Grenade (Ultimate)
This ultimate ability allows Caustic to launch a noxious grenade, On impact, it explodes and clouds the immediate area in a poisonous gas, which will cause damage to enemies over a sustained period.

HOW TO USE

Caustic's lack of direct offensive abilities means that he is best utilised as a crafty support character. He can pin down enemies in his toxic clouds and force them to break cover or divert course. Much like Bloodhound, he can spot enemies under certain conditions – in this case as they pass through his gas traps, so he's very effective at enabling tagging and callouts.

Confusing the opposition by shooting canisters and causing a panic is a great way to herd them into areas where your teammates await. However, flying canisters and massive poison clouds can cause confusion among your own ranks too, so make sure that you're communicating effectively about what you're doing and pinging enemies using Nox Vision.

GIBRALTAR

TANK

PROFILE

Real Name: Makoa Gibraltar
Age: 30

Caught in a mudslide while joyriding with his boyfriend, Gibraltar's father came to his rescue, but wasn't able to save his arm. Makoa never forgave himself and vowed to use his second chance to rescue others using his shields, and a little charm too!

STRENGTHS

+ Shielding yourself and your team with Dome of Protection can give you some much-needed respite.

WEAKNESSES

− His large stature makes him a walking target. Make sure you're always aiming down scopes to limit his vulnerability.

SKILLS

Gun Shield (Passive)
Whenever you aim down the sights of a gun, a shield is deployed to absorb incoming fire, though it's fairly small.

Dome of Protection (Active)
Gibraltar unleashes a dome-shield that lasts for 15 second, allowing the whole team to take shelter from enemy fire.

Defensive Bombardment (Ultimate)
Similarly to Bangalore's ultimate, Gibraltar can also call in a devastating airstrike. Gibraltar throws a smoke signal to mark a location, which is subjected to concentrated mortar fire.

HOW TO USE

Gibraltar is difficult to kill, despite being a large target. This is mostly thanks to his multiple shields and short cooldown period for Dome of Protection. It can also be used to protect teammates, but beware when it runs out, as your squad will all be exposed in a tight pack.

It's always tempting to use Gibraltar to soak up bullets while your teammates flank around but give him a sniper rifle and he becomes a shielded turret. If you're aiming down the scope, enemy shots will deflect off the gun shield. His ultimate is also great at flushing out enemies from cover or pinning them down, but if you can score some direct hits, the damage from the mortar strike will make light work of your enemy.

LIFELINE

MEDIC

PROFILE

Real Name: Ajay Che
Age: 24

Ajay rebelled against her money-hungry parents who were profiting from war and injury. She began devoting her time to helping and healing others in the Apex Games. All she wants is peace across the universe.

STRENGTHS

+ Faster healing times ensure you and your team can get back into the action more quickly.

WEAKNESSES

— Being such a useful Legend means that enemy teams often seek out Lifeline and eliminate her first.

SKILLS

Combat Medic (Passive)
Revive knocked down teammates quicker if Lifeline is protected by a shield. Healing items are applied 25% faster than normal.

D.O.C. Heal Drone (Active)
Once the Drone of Compassion is deployed, it automatically heals teammates in Lifeline's vicinity over time.

Care Package (Ultimate)
Lifeline's ultimate ability is a great way for your squad to get a bunch of items. She calls in a special drop pod that contains a selection of random defensive items for you and your team to utilise.

HOW TO USE

Probably the most important Legend to have on your team because of her healing abilities. Use the D.O.C. as often as possible to ensure you and your team stay healthy. Your ultimate should be deployed as soon as it's ready so your team can benefit from a defensive gear drop.

It's best to keep Lifeline at mid-range so she can be close enough to your team to be able to help out with some long shots and healing, but far enough away that she won't attract all of the enemy's attention. Be ready to rush in and revive your teammates – when Lifeline revives she receives a shield to protect her and her teammate while the revive bar fills. You might want Gibraltar around to throw down a shield in the meantime to protect her.

MIRAGE

DIVERSIONARY

PROFILE

Real Name: Elliott Witt
Age: 30

Mirage takes very little in life seriously, aside from his holographic technology and his brothers. His sense of humour and need for attention shows in his abilities and attitude. Elliott is the rogue of Apex and plays the role perfectly.

STRENGTHS

+ Clones = chaos. They can draw enemy fire when used wisely, allowing a sneaky escape or flanking move.

WEAKNESSES

– None of his abilities cause any damage, which means his offence relies on the random weapons he finds.

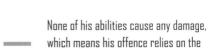

SKILLS

Encore! (Passive)
As a final trick when knocked down, Mirage drops a decoy version of himself, which will sow a seed of doubt that he was ever defeated ...

Psyche Out (Active)
Mirage deploys an identical holographic decoy of himself to distract enemies, allowing him to make a sneaky escape.

Vanishing Act (Ultimate)
It'll be no surprise that Mirage's ultimate ability also relies on decoys. However, this skill is slightly different as it cloaks Mirage and makes him invisible, then sends decoys out in all directions.

HOW TO USE

Mirage is not much of a team player as all of his abilities revolve around confusion tactics, which are often only employed to save his own skin, although he can easily create a diversion to open up attacking possibilities. His ultimate is ideally used when you need to leave an area swiftly as it makes it very tough for the enemy to keep track of where you are and where you're headed.

Well-timed clones can cause mayhem for others on the field, allowing for some more tactical approaches that can lead to satisfying eliminations. Mirage can be one of the more fun characters to use, simply because he is so different from all the others, but his inclusion on a team isn't as vital as some of the other Legends.

OCTANE

QUICK ATTACK

PROFILE

Real Name: Octavio Silva
Age: 24

This death-defying daredevil tried to finish a race for his fans by using a grenade to reach the finish line. After losing his legs, Octavio turned to Lifeline, who fitted him with new robotic limbs. His old stunts no longer thrilled him, so he entered the Apex battlefield.

STRENGTHS

+ He has the ability to constantly heal, increase mobility and aid his team in travelling great distances.

WEAKNESSES

– Octane is quite well-rounded, the only real downside is that you have to sacrifice health for increased speed.

SKILLS

Swift Mend (Passive)
Will constantly restore Octane's health during battle as long as he isn't under attack by an enemy. No medkits necessary!

Stim (Active)
Octane can sacrifice 10 points of health in order to move 30% faster than his normal speed for up to six seconds.

Launch Pad (Ultimate)
Octane's ultimate ability allows him to throw down a jump pad. This allows anyone who comes across it, enemies included, to launch into the air and quickly leap across the King's Canyon map.

HOW TO USE

Octane is fast. Not just a bit faster than everyone else, but 30% faster. His boost of speed makes him a very tricky target for opponents. While you trade off ten points of health for six seconds of extra speed, that health is easily regained by the Passive ability, Swift Mend – as long as you aren't taking fire. With just a two second cooldown, this ability makes for some chaotic moments.

This Legend, brought into the game for Season 1 is there to frustrate others. Combining his movement speed and ultimate ability to drop launch pads, he rarely stands still and is best used in support. His ability to flank enemies at speed is unrivalled; pair him with Mirage and you're sure to bring fun and lunacy to the battlefield.

PATHFINDER

SCOUT

PROFILE

Real Name: MRVN
Age: Unknown

Pathfinder is a Mobile Robotic Versatile eNtity, designed to scout new lands. MRVN has no idea who he is, or who made him, so his mission is to find out. His optimism and open nature makes him a good friend ... but that doesn't mean you can cross him!

STRENGTHS

+ Being able to see how The Ring will move and relocate your team can save a match or tip the scales in your favour.

WEAKNESSES

– Lack of offensive abilities limits Pathfinder's damage potential to just the standard guns and grenades.

SKILLS

Insider Knowledge (Passive)
This skill allows Pathfinder to scan a survey beacon to find out where The Ring will move to next and give your team a head start.

Grappling Hook (Active)
Increase Pathfinder's movement range by launching a hook to drag him across great distances or to high vantage points.

Zipline Gun (Ultimate)
Pathfinder unleashes a zipline between two points. The zipline can be used by your whole team so that you can quickly relocate across the map, and reach strategic areas before your enemies.

HOW TO USE

A true scout can move around with freedom and scope out the lay of the land. Pathfinder's abilities will keep your team moving and ahead of the closing ring. It's a great starter character as you can escape battles easily if things are going awry. If you're feeling overwhelmed, you can use your grapple hook to dash out of trouble.

Knowing where The Ring will move to is always a helpful skill for your team as you can plan your endgame movement in advance. Paired with Bloodhound, you can work together to build a tactical plan of action. The Zipline Gun ultimate is a great tool for the team to move position should you need to wait out the game or find fresher ground for looting.

WRAITH

AVOIDANCE

PROFILE

Real Name: Unknown
Age: Unknown

Wraith has no idea who she truly is. After waking up in a hospital with no memory of her life, she heard voices within her mind. Listening to these new whisperings, Wraith began to harness new powers, determined to find out the truth of her past.

STRENGTHS

+ Voices from the Void can save your life if you find yourself with nobody watching your back.

WEAKNESSES

– When in void-space, you won't be able to pick up items and or even see enemies. Time its use wisely.

Voices from the Void (Passive)
A voice warns Wraith of any approaching dangers. Treat it as an extension of the on-screen radar, not a replacement.

Into the Void (Active)
Wraith conjures and enters an opening in void-space, allowing her to travel undetected around the map to catch enemies by surprise.

Dimensional Rift (Ultimate)
Wraith creates portals linked through void-space, which stay open for 60 seconds. She can exploit the portals to bounce back and forth between two points, allowing her to jump in and out of battle.

HOW TO USE

Wraith's abilities are designed to extend your movement and travel unseen. Her active ability allows her to turn partially invisible for a short time, very helpful for escaping trouble. She won't be able to shoot in this mode, however, so it's best used for covert movement and escapes.

Her ultimate is incredibly helpful for moving your team across great distances, but you'll need to plan its use before activating. Constructing the two portals will allow your team to effectively vanish and appear elsewhere on the map, which is great for the latter stages of the match. Wraith is ideal for a starting player because she is easy to pick up and control and once you've mastered her, she's a constant danger.

WEAPONS

There's an arsenal of exotic weapons available in Apex Legends, which let you eliminate enemy squads in a variety of ways. From the understated pistols and punchy shotguns to the relentless assault rifles, there's a weapon to fit your play-style.

The best way to learn each weapon is to use them – each gun has varying damage stats, magazine sizes (how many bullets it can hold), reload speeds and bullet spread (the random direction bullets fire). Try them all out, test each with all kinds of attachments and talk to your team to see if your choice of weapon complements the ones they tend to favour – you wouldn't want your whole squad to be rocking sniper rifles. If you want to know the difference between your Mozambique and your Mastiff or Hemlock and Havoc, we've got you covered.

ASSAULT RIFLES

The assault rifle is the go-to weapon for damage. It's a great weapon to have equipped most of the time due to its range, damage potential and general ease of use. Each variation is quick to draw and aim, allowing for rapid response to enemy encounters.

HEMLOCK

The Hemlock shoots in bursts every time you pull the trigger, which takes time to get used to. It's fast and if you're accurate you can spit out damage at a rapid rate. However, the relatively low damage ability across distance means that there are other assault rifles that excel at longer ranges.

VK-47 FLATLINE

A fast-firing weapon with mid-range damage, the Flatline isn't the weakest of the bunch, but it won't halt enemies in their tracks. Its reload is swift and it's easy to handle, so it's a good weapon for the opening minutes of a match, but you'll soon want to upgrade.

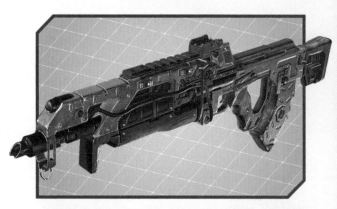

R-301 CARBINE

Many players favour the Carbine over other rifles due to its low recoil, fast firing and power at all ranges. Because the Carbine trades in some damage for an increased rate of fire, it comes a close second to the lethal Havoc when it's equipped with the right attachment.

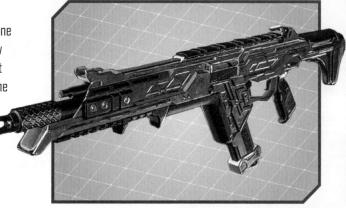

HAVOC

Our pick for the best assault rifle is this beast. While it takes time to get going without the Turbocharger 'hop up', enemies won't stand a chance once it is. A high damage output and hefty clip size make light work of squads.

SMGs

The sub-machine gun (SMG) is designed to perform well at short- and mid-range. In close quarters they can unload clips at an alarming rate, but as your opponent gets further away, you'll need something more accurate, where the shots don't spread as much.

PROWLER

Our top choice from the available SMGs is the Prowler, particularly with the Selectfire Receiver attached. With this boost, it's a reliable damage-dealer when used at close-range. Even without it, the Prowler is a strong damage-per-second (DPS) contender.

ALTERNATOR

For the Alternator to come close to being a great weapon it needs to be kitted out with several attachments, like a mag upgrade and a scope. Without these, it has a good reload speed, which makes it good for starters, but you'll want to upgrade quickly.

R-99

There's a crazy amount of recoil on this gun, so if you find one you better start looking for a barrel attachment. The fast fire rate does make the R-99 a high-damage choice, but the real trouble will be keeping your target in the crosshairs.

LMGs

Let's be honest, there are only two Light Machine Guns (LMG) in Apex Legends and they're both excellent. They share a high damage output and increased accuracy on their SMG cousins, but they can be a drain on your ammo sources.

DEVOTION

As it consumes plenty of energy ammo, the Devotion often means you'll spend more time looting to keep it loaded than you would like. However, the fire-rate will cause massive damage over a short amount of time, which makes it a great option.

SPITFIRE

There's not much between the LMGs, but it's hard not to favour the Spitfire. It's more accurate than the Devotion, has great damage stats and the ammo clip is huge. The heavy rounds it uses are more easily found around King's Canyon too.

SNIPER RIFLES

Probably the most skill-based weapon in Apex Legends, the Sniper takes practice to use effectively. Keep a lead on your target by aiming your sights slightly ahead of where an enemy is moving and soon you'll be nailing 100-metre headshots.

KRABER .50 CAL

The Kraber is so powerful that it can eliminate enemies with one hit. However, it's a legendary weapon, so it's hard to find and you can't add any attachments. With a limited clip too, its best for taking out knocked enemies.

LONGBOW DMR

The Longbow is our top sniper, if only for how easy it is to find around King's Canyon. It can't fire as quickly as the Scout, but it can cause more damage. If you're accurate with sniper rifles, this is a great choice – add a 'hop up' to increase the headshot damage.

G7 SCOUT

The name gives away the Scout's versatility. It's quick fire-rate makes it useful at shorter distances, though it does lack in damage slightly. It's great for racing around and 'scouting' an area out, but for lethality, go elsewhere.

TRIPLE TAKE

Oddly for a sniper rifle, the Triple Take isn't great at long ranges. It fires a burst of three rounds instead of one. At shorter ranges, it can land all three shots for insane damage, but at distance, the shots spread too much, It's best to pick a traditional sniper rifle.

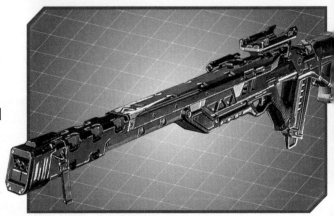

SHOTGUNS

Close-quarters only, these weapons are by far the deadliest in one-on-one scenarios. Accuracy is key here if you want each shot to count – aim wildly and you will lose the fight every time. Learn the recoil and bullet spreads to make sure you survive the odds.

MOZAMBIQUE
Widely regarded as the worst weapon in the game, the Mozambique is discarded for basically any other weapon. It has little power and a terrible bullet spray, even for a shotgun, but it's better than being unarmed ... just about.

EVA-8 AUTO
A great starter weapon for new players, the EVA-8 is a forgiving gun for those getting to grips with the controls. What it lacks in damage output, it makes up for in fire-rate, and the bullet spread guarantees that at least some of your shots will land.

MASTIFF
Found only through supply drops, the Mastiff is one of few legendary weapons. It uses unique ammo that can't be found on the battlefield, giving you only twenty shots. However it has the highest damage, so it's possible to knock enemies with a single shot.

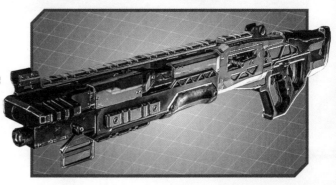

PEACEKEEPER

A great all-rounder, the Peacekeeper was so good that it was nerfed shortly before Season 1 started. That still hasn't made it any less popular though – with a few choice attachments, this weapon can be a thorn in any enemy's side.

PISTOLS

Often overlooked by players as 'default' weapons, pistols can be surprisingly powerful and have plenty to offer. They may not be the most exciting weapon, but being able to pull a quick sidearm can mean the difference between being eliminated and staying alive.

P2020

A run-of-the-mill sidearm that doesn't have the capacity to cause too much bother. It's weak and demands accuracy from players, otherwise you're bound to be caught short. It can get you out of a bind if you're desperate, but there are better pistols and better weapons to keep hold of.

WINGMAN

A pistol rarely makes the list of 'must-haves', but the Wingman is a phenomenon. It has incredible damage, even at longer ranges, and a great rate-of-fire. Add a Skullpiercer hop-up to cause more headshot damage and it becomes one of the most powerful weapons in the game.

RE-45 AUTO

An automatic weapon is only as good as your aim. The RE-45 Auto sprays rounds at great pace, but you'll need to make sure that you keep the crosshairs trained on an enemy so that damage hits home. It's best used with a magazine attachment, which will increase the clip size and allowing you to shoot off more rounds before reloading.

ACCESSORIES

There are many attachments to find around King's Canyon, and each one boosts the way a gun handles and performs. If you hover over an attachment on the ground, you can see if it'll work with your gun and picking it up will equip it automatically. Attachments also come in varying rarities, so it's worth upgrading them if you get the chance.

HOP UP

A 'hop up' can only be fitted to particular guns and isn't interchangeable. For example, an attachment for the Peacekeeper can't be added to the Havoc. What these items do differs greatly. Rather than boosting a base stat, they will add more of a perk to the gun instead.

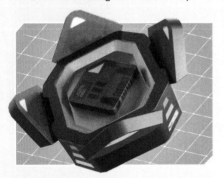

PRECISION CHOKE
Creates a tighter bullet spray for the Peacekeeper and Triple Take.

SKULLPIERCER RIFLING
Increases the headshot damage for the Longbow and Wingman.

SELECTFIRE RECEIVER
Allows the Havoc and Prowler to auto-fire when the trigger is pulled.

TURBOCHARGER
Decreases the spin-up time for Devotion and Havoc weapons.

MAGAZINES

A magazine upgrade usually increases ammo capacity, allowing you to fire the weapon for longer before reloading. As you can see below, the magazine upgrades here also boost other stats, too.

EXTENDED HEAVY MAG
Available for 'heavy weapons'. Increases ammo capacity for all rarity levels and reduces reload speed for everything but Common weapons.

EXTENDED LIGHT MAG
Available for 'light weapons'. Increases ammo capacity for all rarity levels and reduces reload speed for everything but Common weapons

SHOTGUN BOLT
For shotguns only. Increases ammo capacity and fire-rate for all rarity levels.

OPTICS

An optic attachment adjusts the zoom and precision of aiming when looking down the sights of a weapon. The zoom distance is often a matter of preference as some people don't feel they need such a close view of their target.

HOLO (1X)
Close-range sight for any weapon.

DIGITAL THREAT (1X)
For Shotguns, SMGs and Pistols; auto-detects threats.

VARIABLE HOLO (1X–2X)
For all weapons; adjustable to two ranges.

HCOG CLASSIC (1X)
Close-range sight for any weapon.

HCOG BRUISER (2X)
Medium-range sight for any weapon.

SNIPER (6X)
Long-range sight for sniper rifles.

VARIABLE SNIPER (4X–8X)
Adjustable sight for sniper rifles.

DIGITAL SNIPER THREAT
Long-range adjustable sight; auto-detects threats.

STOCKS

Stock upgrades come in two varieties – Standard Stock and Sniper Stock. Both variations reduce the time it takes for you to draw your weapon, and reduce the aim drift you have when looking down the scope of the gun.

BARREL STABLILIZER

There is only one barrel attachment available and it fits most LMGs, SMGs and assault rifles. The Barrel Stabilizer reduces weapon recoil, allowing you to keep you aim steady. The Legendary variant also reduces muzzle flash, meaning people won't see the bright pop of bullets leaving your gun.

ITEMS AND ARMOUR

Although the stats for each Legend in the game are the same, you can find items throughout King's Canyon to replenish health or add armour to your character and increase their power. As well as your standard health items, shields are a must-grab if you can find them. They add an extra layer of hit points and can more easily be recharged.

There are many ways to heal your character during the battle. We've broken down the different items and how much health they replenish.

SYRINGE
Restores 25 health

MED KIT
Restores 100 health

SHIELD CELL
Restores 25 shield

SHIELD BATTERY
Restores 100 shield

PHOENIX KIT
Restores 100 health
and 100 shield

ULTIMATE ACCELERANT
Restores 20% ultimate

Quality of gear is marked out by colour, which is consistent across all gear in Apex Legends. No matter whether you pick up a helmet or a backpack, the colour will give a quick indication of how good the item is.

GEAR

White signifies the most basic gear, while blue items are slightly improved and slightly rarer. Purple items are Epic must-haves, and Legendary items are golden and provide significant boosts. As rarity increases, so does the quality of the item. For example, a White knockdown shield has just 100 hit points, whereas an Epic rarity of the same item has 750 hit points.

BODY SHIELDS

These are your basic shield, which is topped up with shield cells and batteries.

Common: +50 shield capacity

Rare: +75 shield capacity

Epic: +100 shield capacity

Legendary: +100 shield capacity; fully recharges shield after you've executed a knocked opponent

KNOCKDOWN SHIELDS

A knockdown shield can be activated once your health depletes and you're 'knocked' to the floor. It creates a shield around you preventing incoming damage. It doesn't, however, stop an enemy from executing you.

Common: 100 health knockdown shield

Rare: 250 health knockdown shield

Epic: 750 health knockdown shield

Legendary: 750 health knockdown shield, plus you can self-revive once

HELMETS

Helmets are another type of armour, but these act as damage modifiers, reducing the amount of damage you will take overall.

Common: 10% damage reduction

Rare: 20% damage reduction

Epic: 25% damage reduction

Legendary: 25% damage reduction, plus increased charge speed for abilities

BACKPACKS

Backpacks simply unlock more slots for you to store items.

Common: +2 inventory slots

Rare: +4 inventory slots

Epic: +6 inventory slots

Legendary: +6 inventory slots, plus healing items take half as long to use

CRAFTING, METALS AND COSMETICS

The currencies and cosmetics in Apex Legends can be quite confusing as they are all used for different things and even overlap each other a little. We've put together a brief outline of what to look out for and what each currency will get you.

RARITY PERCENTAGES

We all love seeing a rare item pop out from a Supply Bin, but just how rare is Rare and how hard is it to find a Legendary weapon? The figures below should give you an idea of how hard it is to find those items.

⬤ 100% – Rare Item or Better   ⬤ 24.8% – Epic or Better   ⬤ 7.4% – Legendary

APEX COINS

These coins are a premium currency that you redeem with real-world money. If you are buying Apex Coins, you must get permission from a parent or guardian to spend the money if you're under 18 years old.

LEGEND TOKENS

Legend Tokens are earned through playing and are used simply for unlocking certain characters – Caustic and Mirage – as well as certain cosmetics.

APEX PACKS

An Apex Pack is where you will find all the exciting cosmetic items to make you stand out from the crowd. You will earn Apex Packs just by levelling up, but you can purchase them using Apex Coins too. When you open a pack, you'll receive three random cosmetic items from the list below:

- Weapon Skins
- Legend Skins
- Legend Finishers
- Banner Frames
- Banner Poses
- Banner Stat Trackers
- Intro Quips
- Elimination Quips
- Crafting Metals

CRAFTING METALS

Crafting metals can only be found within Apex Packs and these are used to unlock standard cosmetics for each Legend. Cosmetics for your favourite Legend can cost anywhere from 30 metals up to 1,200 metals.

The number of metals you'll receive will depend on the rarity drop:

- Common crafting metal = 15
- Rare crafting metal = 30
- Epic crafting metal = 200
- Legendary crafting metal = 600

REVIVING YOUR TEAMMATES

Reviving a teammate in Apex Legends is easy, though not without its risks. When a squad member is knocked down ('knocked'), they rely on others to help them get back in the fight. In order to help a buddy, simply approach their body and hold down the interact button. When the revive bar is full, your ally will rise with a small amount of their health. If you can't revive or reach them in time, they will bleed out and be eliminated from the game.

REVIVAL TIPS

- Stay aware of your surroundings. While reviving a friend you are unable to shoot, doing so means resetting that revive progress bar.

- When knocked you can still move, although rather slowly. Find a place to hide and wait for rescue. You can still open and close doors so find shelter.

- Communication is just as important when knocked. Crucially, you can still ping enemies when laid out so you can warn them of danger while they're focused on getting you up.

CAN I REVIVE MYSELF?

Only with a very rare item – a Legendary knockdown shield. As with other knockdown shields, this will protect you while laid out. However, it will also revive you much like a teammate would. Of course, something this strong can only be used once and will revert to a Rare knockdown shield upon use.

RESPAWNING

Apex Legends allows you to respawn and rejoin the fight rather than heading back to the title screen. When a teammate is downed, they will drop a crate, leaving behind their items and weapons but also a banner. By collecting this banner, you can bring your downed ally back into the game, but you need to go a little out of your way to help. Take the banner to one of the respawn beacons dotted around the map – they're red and have little holograms on the top. These beacons are also visible on your map as green diamonds.

RESPAWN TIPS

- Grab that banner quickly, it disappears after 90 seconds meaning your friend stays dead and out of the game. As long as someone on the team has picked up the banner, any teammate can respawn you.

- Beacons are not randomly placed, so you can learn their locations over time and repeated plays.

- When your squadmate respawns, they're brought back via a drop-pod. This will alert enemies in the area to your position, so beware.

DO I KEEP MY GEAR WHEN I RESPAWN?

Sadly not. Respawning effectively means starting from scratch, so you'll need to hunt down some weapons and items fast, hope that your helpful teammate hands you a spare weapon to keep you going, or reach the crate you dropped when you died.

JUMP TOWERS AND TRAVERSAL

SLIDING

Sliding is a simple technique for movement and can save your skin in tight situations. To initiate a slide, all you need to do is hold down the crouch button while you're sprinting.

After a second, you'll reach your maximum speed for a slide. Take some time to practise your sliding – learn how long it takes to aim when you stop, try strafing left and right as you slide and try combinations of sliding and sprinting, to get used to the movement of your character.

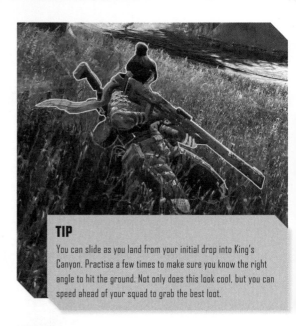

TIP

You can slide as you land from your initial drop into King's Canyon. Practise a few times to make sure you know the right angle to hit the ground. Not only does this look cool, but you can speed ahead of your squad to grab the best loot.

CLIMBING

Handy for creeping up on enemies looking into the distance from their perches, climbing is as simple as walking towards a wall and jumping at it. Your character will begin climbing to the top of the structure automatically, just keep holding forward. It's great for reaching tricky spots on the map or finding little areas to recoup health after a fight.

ZIPLINES AND BALLOONS

Other than climbing and sliding, you'll be able to traverse King's Canyon with the ziplines dotted around. Some go across gaps, some go vertically and some have a balloon on top.

TIP
The interact button that gets you onto one of these lines will also launch you off of them at great speed as well.

With horizontal ziplines you'll notice that you're a bit of a sitting duck as you whizz along to your destination. The ones that go up and down are great for quick escapes or gaining the all-important high ground. Ziplines with balloons at the top will launch you into the air at their summit, allowing you to deploy your rockets, much like when you first drop into King's Canyon.

BOOST JUMPING

This is one of the more advanced techniques for moving around King's Canyon, but once you've learned it, you'll never stop using it.

As you're running, you'll need to start sliding, just for a very short time – less than a second – before hitting the jump button. Doing this takes advantage of the extra momentum from the slide and launches you further into the jump. Jump too early or too late and you won't notice that boost, but once you've nailed it, you can start using it to gain ground on enemies.

SUPPLY SHIPS AND HOT ZONES

King's Canyon is full to the brim with loot, which presents itself in many ways. Of course, you want the best loot possible to get the upper hand in battle, so raid the standard Supply Bins scattered all over the map as the first port of call after dropping. If you want that really good loot, the kind that will make your enemies quake, then look no further.

SUPPLY SHIPS

At the start of your match, open up the map and look out for a ship outlined in blue. This is a supply ship, and on board you will find lots of rare loot. It's entirely possible to land here right from the initial drop and tool up for the fight, but, as with all lucrative areas, they will be swarming with opponents.

While you can land on the moving ship, it's safer and far easier to wait until it has docked. Of course, all the loot could be gone by then though, so you need to weigh up your options. Other ships will spawn throughout the match and can be accessed when they reach the end of their journey via ziplines.

HOT ZONES

Hot zones are like the supply ships in that they are designated at the start of the match by a blue circle on the map. You're guaranteed great loot, but also competition from your enemies. If you're dropping here, make sure you do so with your squad for the best chance of survival.

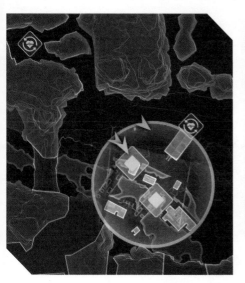

SUPPLY DROPS

These falling treasures will randomly drop to the ground with a bounty of loot. The great thing about these drops is they can fall anywhere in King's Canyon, and you'll always find three pieces of high-quality gear. There's also a slight chance of finding a Legendary weapon too. These drops are the only way to get your hands on the Kraber .50-CAL or the Mastiff, so keep your eyes open!

LOOT TICKS

A loot tick is a small robot that is often hidden from plain sight. You'll know you're close to a tick when you hear unusual mechanical sounds nearby. Follow the noise to find a triangular robot on skinny legs, in varying rarity colours. Simply damage it to release the loot.

WORKING AS A TEAM

There is no solo mode in Apex Legends, so every match focuses on the team experience. Working together effectively is integral to securing a win so you must be a team-player. Whether you're jumping into King's Canyon with friends or strangers, there are lots of ways to communicate and work together to grab a victory.

PINGS

Apex utilises a ping system that helps you communicate with party members. You can ping almost anything, from enemies to loot locations – you can even request a heal. Take time to look through the different pings available and remember the quick actions to bring them into play.

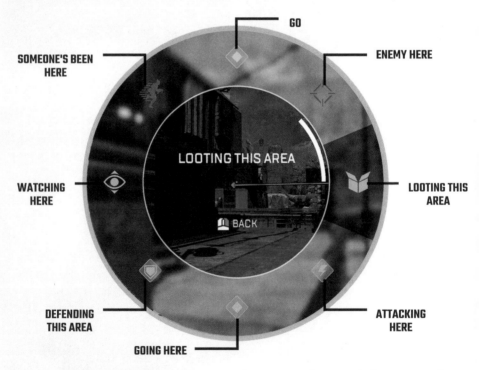

GO

SOMEONE'S BEEN HERE

ENEMY HERE

WATCHING HERE

LOOTING THIS AREA

LOOTING THIS AREA

BACK

DEFENDING THIS AREA

ATTACKING HERE

GOING HERE

As well as using the basic pings, you can ping any object you see, from supply drops to specific weapons. These are called contextual pings, and they can be performed by pressing the ping button while aiming at objects in the game.

CALL-OUTS

Call-outs are verbal shouts to describe points on the map, enemies and loot locations. While the developers obviously name specific areas of the map, players soon begin giving them nicknames or shortened versions. It's worth listening out for and learning these so you can communicate info as quickly as possible.

COMPASS

Always be aware of the compass at the top of the screen. Much like learning call-outs for locations, the numbers on the compass can be equally helpful when communicating. As well as pinging an enemy, you can describe where they are and be more specific. You can call out the number on the compass when aiming at an enemy to give allies an idea of distance, This is also helpful if you're in the middle of a fight and see another group of enemies moving on your position. A quick call of the compass numbers will help everyone build a mental map.

SHARING

Don't hoard good weapons just because they're good weapons. There's no point in holding onto a Rare sniper rifle if your skills aren't great. You should always practise with new weapons, but if you have an expert sniper on your team, hand it over. The same goes for items – if you have a Lifeline on your team, they should have lots of med kits, as they can heal a teammate faster.

TIP
Remember to update your teammates with what items and weapons you're finding, especially if you don't want to use them.

MOVEMENT

When possible, try to move as a team or at least keep tabs on where your squadmates are. Watch their backs and cover them if they're making a dash for loot. Try not to run off from your team – if they have to search for you after you've been knocked, they won't be happy. It's always better to divert the whole team in the hunt for better gear, than to venture out on your own.

PICK FOR THE TEAM

When it comes to picking your character, you'll always want to choose someone you enjoy playing as. However, it's good to keep in mind characters that work well together so you have a balance in your squad. Try to play as lots of different characters, especially when playing with friends. You can learn new tricks and new ways to support each other, which will benefit everyone.

LEGEND COMBOS

Finding the right dynamic between your team is just as important as how you play during the match, so get familiar with the strengths and weaknesses of every Legend as soon as possible. To help you along the way, we've come up with a handful of excellent combos that you could include in your team. Pick these characters, work together and you're likely to come out on top.

PATHFINDER X CAUSTIC

Use Caustic's gas clouds to damage enemies, which will automatically reveal their location. Pathfinder can then set up a zipline so the rest of the squad can reach the enemies and ambush them.

GIBRALTAR X WRAITH

Gibraltar can drop a Dome-Shield which will draw enemy fire as they try to break it down. This gives Wraith a chance to jump through Void-Space and discreetly flank the enemy while they're distracted.

BANGALORE X MIRAGE

A good way to retreat is to have Bangalore pop smoke grenades in the surrounding area. While the smoke is clearing, Mirage can leave behind plenty of clones to leave the enemy guessing.

BATTLE PASS

A new season starts every three months in Apex Legends, and with each season comes a new Battle Pass, which offers many cosmetic upgrades, new weapons, plenty of balancing behind the scenes and even new playable characters – Octane was the first additional character released as part of Season 1. Let's take a look at how the Battle Pass works.

SEASON PROGRESS

In this box you'll find all the details about the current seasons and your advancement in it. It has the season number and name, the time left, the level you've reached and the experience you've earned during the current season.

REWARD SHOWCASE

When you highlight an option on the Battle Pass tiers, you'll see a preview of the reward in this area. It will allow you to see skins, frames and trackers you'll unlock, and listen to any quips.

BATTLE PASS TIERS

The row at the bottom shows a selection of levels around your current level, and the rewards that unlock at each tier. You can scroll through the rewards for the whole season.

NAVIGATION TABS

These tabs will take you to different parts of the lobby. Play will drop you into a match, Legends is where you can view all of the characters, while the Armory lets you check weapons and skins you've unlocked. Battle Pass shows your season progress and Store is where you can purchase more Apex Coins or bundles.

CURRENCIES

This part of the screen shows how much of each currency you have. The blue icon is crafting materials, the red icon is Legend Tokens, and the yellow icon is Apex Coins.

BUYING A BATTLE PASS

The standard Battle Pass costs 950 Apex Coins and requires players to start at tier one. Levelling up through the earning of XP unlocks new cosmetic items that can be applied to your favourite Legend. You can also purchase the Battle Pass Bundle for 2800 Apex Coins. This gets you all the rewards from the first 25 tiers and boosts your season progress. Note that you can still unlock some rewards without purchasing a Battle Pass.

TIER REWARDS

As you level up through the Battle Pass, you'll unlock more and more new items that will allow you to customise your Legends and the way your game looks. Take a glance below to discover all the goodies waiting for you in the Wild Frontier Battle Pass.

SKINS

The Battle Pass starts off with unique skins that are only available for a season. The first tier of Season 1 rewarded players with unique themed skins for Lifeline, Mirage and Wraith.

WEAPON SKINS

As well as being able to customise your Legend's appearance, the Battle Pass affords many opportunities to freshen up your lethal arsenal with weapon skins.

QUIPS

These unique unlocks are funny phrases that your Legend utters when they enter a battle, are observed in the menu, or when they defeat an enemy.

BADGES

Though they serve no greater purpose than show off your achievements, these badges can be applied to your account to show how far you advance within any given season.

FRAMES

Another way to show the world how well you've advanced through a season, frames appear at the start of a battle and hold your chosen Legend and stat trackers.

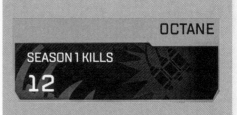

STAT TRACKERS

These widgets allow you to showcase the stats that you want people to see. If you've been racking up the kills with Octane, you can show off that exact stat.

APEX COINS

You can earn Apex Coins just by playing the game! If you save all the Apex Coins you receive from a Battle Pass during a season, you'll have enough to buy next season's Pass!

BOOSTS

If progress is slow, never fear – there are multiple rewards that increase experience by 5% when you play with friends. You and your squad will soon be speeding through the tiers.

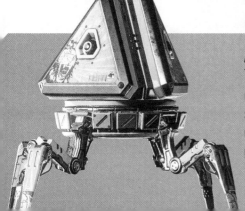

APEX PACKS

These bundles are premium packages that contain a random selection of items, from skins and quips to coins and frames. They come in different varieties, but you're guaranteed one rare item per pack.

ONLINE SAFETY

Apex Legends features a more realistic visual style compared to similar games and is rated as suitable for players 16 years of age and over by PEGI. We've put together some simple rules to help you stay safe and keep the internet an awesome place to spend time.

GENERAL ONLINE SAFETY

 Never give out your real name – don't use it as your username.

Never give out any of your personal details.

Never tell anybody your password.

Take regular breaks from playing.

Always report any incidence of cheating or harassment.

ONLINE CHAT

In Apex Legends, there is live, unmoderated voice chat between users. You can navigate to the Settings section in the lobby, select the Audio tab, and reduce the Voice Chat Volume down to 0 to turn off any voice chat from any player. You can still communicate with the Ping system.

If you would like to keep voice chat on, but don't want to hear from certain individuals, you can do that too. Open your inventory during a match and scroll to the Squad tab. Find the player that you want to mute and select the speaker icon beneath their image.

SOCIAL MEDIA SCAMS

There are many accounts on social media sites like Facebook and Twitter that claim to give away free Apex Coins and other currencies, which will be transferred to their account. Be sceptical – it's important to check the authenticity of these accounts and offers before giving away personal information.

SOUND

Apex Legends is a game where sound is crucial. Players will often wear headphones, meaning parents won't be able to hear what is being said by strangers. Set up your console or computer to have sound coming from the TV as well as the headset so you can hear what other players are saying to your child.

SCREEN TIME

Taking regular breaks is important. Set play sessions by using a timer. However, Apex Legends games can last up to 30 minutes and if your child finishes playing in the middle of a round, they'll leave their teammates a person short and lose any points they've earned. It's advisable to give advanced warning for stopping play.

IN-GAME PURCHASES

Apex Legends does offer the ability to make in-game purchases such as the Battle Pass and cosmetic skins, but they're not required to play the game. They also don't improve a player's performance.

PARENTAL CONTROLS

Apex Legends doesn't have any parental controls due to its PEGI 16 rating. If your suitably-aged child is playing the game, exercise caution and check in regularly to make sure you know how and with whom they're playing.

SIGN OFF

Apex Legends has emerged and garnered a huge audience in record time. It forces players to learn a few more intricacies than others in the genre and we hope that with our help you become a better player and, more importantly, a great teammate.

We've taken you through everything from where and how to land, how each character fits into a team and noted some of the best (and worst) weapons in the game. As with any videogame, Apex Legends is, above all else, about having fun. Among the guns, items, abilities and skills, we hope that you can work together with your chosen squad to become the best that you can be.

Learn, improvise and talk to others about how to be a better player. Let us know where you're dropping and we'll keep a Wingman ready for you when you respawn.

We'll see you in King's Canyon.